Boris Johnson's Brilliant Plan For Brexit

TABLE OF CONTENTS

CHAPTER 1

NOTHING

NOTHING

NOTHING

NOTHING

NOTHING

NOTHING

NOTHING

NOTHING

NOTHING

NOTHING

CHAPTER 2

NOTHING

NOTHING

NOTHING

NOTHING

NOTHING

NOTHING

NOTHING

NOTHING

NOTHING

NOTHING

CHAPTER 3

NOTHING

NOTHING

NOTHING

NOTHING

NOTHING

NOTHING

NOTHING

NOTHING

NOTHING

NOTHING

CHAPTER 4

NOTHING

NOTHING

NOTHING

NOTHING

NOTHING

NOTHING

NOTHING

NOTHING

NOTHING

NOTHING

CHAPTER 5

NOTHING

NOTHING

NOTHING

NOTHING

NOTHING

NOTHING

NOTHING

NOTHING

NOTHING

NOTHING

CHAPTER 6

NOTHING

NOTHING

NOTHING

NOTHING

NOTHING

NOTHING

NOTHING

NOTHING

NOTHING

NOTHING

CHAPTER 7

NOTHING

NOTHING

NOTHING

NOTHING

NOTHING

NOTHING

NOTHING

NOTHING

NOTHING

NOTHING

CHAPTER 8

NOTHING

NOTHING

NOTHING

NOTHING

NOTHING

NOTHING

NOTHING

NOTHING

NOTHING

NOTHING

CHAPTER 9

NOTHING

NOTHING

NOTHING

NOTHING

NOTHING

NOTHING

NOTHING

NOTHING

NOTHING

NOTHING

CHAPTER 10

NOTHING

NOTHING

NOTHING

NOTHING

NOTHING

NOTHING

NOTHING

NOTHING

NOTHING

NOTHING

CHAPTER 11

NOTHING

NOTHING

NOTHING

NOTHING

NOTHING

NOTHING

NOTHING

NOTHING

NOTHING

NOTHING

CHAPTER 12

NOTHING

NOTHING

NOTHING

NOTHING

NOTHING

NOTHING

NOTHING

NOTHING

NOTHING

NOTHING